ADVENTURE EVERYWHERE

ADVENTURE EVERYWHERE

Pablo Picasso's Paris Nightlife

DAVE HASLAM

First published in the UK in 2023 by Cōnfingō Publishing

249 Burton Road, Didsbury, Manchester, M20 2WA
www.confingopublishing.uk

Cover design by Zoë McLean
Typesetting by John Oakey

Printed by TJ Books Limited

A CIP catalogue record for this book is available from the British Library

ISBN 978-1-7399614-9-7

2 4 6 8 10 9 7 5 3 1

To Tim, with thanks.

Pablo Picasso and his friend Carles Casagemas arrived at the Gare d'Orsay from Barcelona in October 1900 just as Picasso was celebrating his nineteenth birthday. Before setting off to Paris they had made arrangements to rent a friend's vacant living space on rue Campagne Première, close to the cemetery in Montparnasse. Once they'd dropped their luggage there, they set off over to see some Catalan friends in Montmartre (way across the other side of the city). It soon became clear to them that they should be staying in Montmartre rather than Montparnasse.

Paris was the epicentre of avant-garde art; in Montmartre there were small but exciting coteries of artists, poets, writers, anarchists, and bohemians of all kinds. Just as appealingly for Picasso and Casagemas, the cost of living in the area was low, rents were cheap, nightlife was exciting and extensive, café owners would extend credit, and in the words of one writer on the period, '*les femmes ne sont pas farouches*' ('the women are not shy').[1]

The two young Spaniards took a room in the heart of Montmartre, at 49 rue Gabrielle, a very short distance from the Moulin de la Galette dance hall on rue Lepic. Within weeks, Casagemas eagerly contacted friends back home with lists of late-night venues he and Picasso had already visited in Montmartre and around the Place Blanche and Place Pigalle on the boulevard de Clichy – the southern edge of Montmartre at its border with Pigalle.

The fortunes of the two friends were to differ hugely. Within six months, Casagemas would take his own life, his predisposition to dark moods exacerbated by an unhinged and unrequited passion for a young woman called Germaine Gargallo. Picasso would make further visits to the city, before settling in Paris, only moving on fifty years later.

Montmartre – which still calls itself a 'village' – is on a small hill (or '*la Butte*' as it's affectionately known). It's a favourite area for tourists in the current era, many of whom make their way to the basilica

---

[1] Gilles Schlesser, *Picasso À Paris* (Parigramme, 2020), 15.

Sacré Cœur at the top of the hill from where there's an astonishing view of Paris. Incorporated into the city only in 1860, Montmartre was at the edge of Paris geographically, economically and politically.

Up until 1912, Picasso lived in various places on the slopes of *la Butte* or close to the Place Pigalle. His many influences, the people he met, the places he visited in the area, all poured into his work; from the most dilapidated brandy-soaked bar to the excitement of evenings at the Cirque Medrano. His very first painting after arriving in Paris featured the Moulin de la Galette. He was tuned into the sights and sounds of life after dark. Guitars sweep through his work, and his 1914 sculptures of a glass of absinthe is a landmark moment in the history of art.

The Moulin de la Galette, just along from Picasso's first home in Montmartre, was originally a mill known for the manufacture of flour for flat brown cakes called *galettes*. In the mid 19th century a space was opened on the site for what was known as a *guinguette*; an open-air pop-up bar. In the summer months on Sundays and holidays, afternoon parties were hosted in this space. The Moulin de la Galette now is a restaurant. There are other café bars, nightclubs or cabarets that have survived in one or way another, including the Moulin Rouge adjacent to Place Blanche.

Higher up the hill, away from the boulevard de Clichy, the surroundings were more rough and rustic. A lawless area, the *maquis*, on the north-western slopes, was a walk on the wild side, flimsy shacks and insanitary alleys, and practically a no-go zone for strangers. In the first decade of the 20th century, a particular breed of violent Parisian bandits became prominent: the Apaches, a collection of criminal gangs famed for their brutality, but also their dandified dress sense. Belleville was more of a home to them than Montmartre though; the bad lads of the *maquis* were less organised and mythologised, but equally violent.

On the other side of the hill from the Moulin Rouge and on the edge of the *maquis*, there's another venue that's survived since Picasso's time: the Lapin Agile. Stand outside the Lapin Agile and look up the hill and you'll see a vineyard to your left. It's one of the last few reminders of how rustic this part of Montmartre was in Picasso's time; famous, or even failed, artists outnumbered by goats, chickens and feral cats.

Picasso was a regular at the Lapin Agile; he'd be there with friends and allies. The host was Frédé Gérard, a recognisable Montmartre character whose first business involved walking the streets with his donkey, selling fish. From there he had progressed to running Zut, a dive of a place which had been one of the first favourite drinking dens frequented by Picasso and Casagemas. Frédé moved on to the Lapin Agile after Zut had been shut by police suspicious of what was said to be the anarchist clientele.

Picasso's early years in Paris were marked by a typically bohemian mix of art, sex, drugs, and bouts of severe poverty. Later, he'd move across the River Seine to more well-to-do neighbourhoods – by that time famous and spending any evenings out at gallery openings or parties alongside fashionistas and social-ites. But in his first decade and a half in Paris, his earn-ings, the preferences of his friends, and his youthful temperament drew him to less glitzy places: down-at-heel bars of the kind we might now describe as 'edgy'. He later looked back on the times with fondness. The simplicity of an irresponsible life.

The Lapin Agile was originally called Cabaret des Assassins (tradition has it that it took this name af-ter a band of assassins broke in and killed the owner's son). A can-can dancer called Adèle Decerf bought it in 1886 but moved on in 1903. Frédé, taking over, was easy-going, something of an enthusiastic amateur art-ist, and also loved to pick up and play his guitar. His donkey was usually tethered outside the Lapin Agile; his other pets, including a crow and a goat, were apparently welcome to put in an appearance in the cabaret if they so desired.

A book entitled *Pleasure Guide to Paris for Bachelors* was published in 1903.[2] It describes several dozen bars, restaurants, theatres and cabaret clubs in Montmartre and Pigalle, many of which would have been familiar to Picasso and his friends. The book warns that the Lapin Agile's surroundings at night are dark and gloomy but that it has a reputation for 'excellent rabbit stew' cooked by Frédé's wife Berthe, and served 'on a rough deal table under the shadow of the large trees or in the spacious dining-room, around which are painted panels, the work of artists of the Butte'.[3] At various times, paintings on the wall included work by Utrillo, Poulbot, and Suzanne Valadon.

On sunny days, Picasso took his dogs up to the *terrasse* outside the Lapin Agile and sat under an acacia tree surrounded by Frédé's pets. In 1904, he painted a subtle pastel and watercolour portrait of the crow being petted by Frédé's daughter Margot.

In 1905, Frédé commissioned a painting by Picasso, perhaps in lieu of paying his bar tab. In the completed work, Frédé is in the background in a

---

[2] George Day, *Pleasure Guide to Paris for Bachelors* (Nilsson and Company, 1903).
[3] Ibid., 107-8.

baggy brown suit playing his guitar, and in the foreground there's a couple sitting at a small table, both with an empty glass in front of them. The woman is wearing an extravagant hat, and dressed in red, with a feather boa. Both are lost in thought; there's no eye contact.

The woman is generally assumed to be Germaine Gargallo. It was his reaction to the failure of his relationship with Germaine that had led to Casagemas taking his life. The other half of the couple is a self-portrait by Picasso, portraying himself as an unsmiling harlequin. Circus performers were a major interest in this period of Picasso's career, at a time when he'd spend many evenings at the Cirque Medrano.

In the aftermath of Casagemas's death Picasso and Germaine Gargallo had a brief sexual relationship. The two had a lot of shared and problematic history. Despite the diamond-shaped splashes of blue, scarlet, and mustard yellow of the harlequin shirt and the colours of Germaine's clothes, the atmosphere of the painting is deeply melancholic. Black lines surround their silhouettes. The couple appear barely connected.

Frédé Gérard's evenings of music, heavy drinking, and poetry would frequently go on through the early hours. The Lapin Agile had a piano, frequently out of tune but nevertheless played with gusto by various performers. The evening's amateur singers would be remunerated by some food and drink and any tips they could solicit from the audience.

Picasso wasn't the only customer at the Lapin Agile who carried a revolver for protection. His crew of artists and poets had a habit of joyfully, drunkenly, firing their revolvers into the air as they left the venue, disturbing any locals with a proper job trying to get some sleep.

+

Less than thirty years before Picasso arrived, Montmartre had been wracked by violent insurrection and mass murder. The Commune was a revolutionary government established in 1871, after France's humiliating defeat in the Franco-Prussian War, as an alternative to the Versailles regime; its base was Montmartre. The Commune asserted women's and workers' rights and the separation of church and state; but within just a couple of months, the uprising collapsed when the French army moved in, crushing the rebels. Over 30,000 Communards were killed by soldiers loyal to Versailles. In one incident, 147 rebel leaders were executed against a wall in the Père Lachaise cemetery.

After suppression of the uprising, on the surface at least France enjoyed a period of political stability from the mid 1870s to the outbreak of World War One, an era that in retrospect has been dubbed *La Belle Époque*. But in so many ways this was, and remains, history laced with artificial sweetener. During the *Belle Époque* the aristocracy benefitted from huge untaxed wealth and privilege; the bourgeoisie enjoyed years of plenty, better food, and beautiful new homes; but the lowest classes continued to be exploited and brutalised.

After the failure of the Commune, Montmartre retained a reputation for radicalism, which took many forms. The area was home to anarchists, some intent on violent anti-government activity while many others harboured considerable sympathy for the rebels (annual demonstrations commemorating the Commune were invariably well attended). *Le Père Peinard* was a weekly anarchist newspaper that relentlessly attacked the political and economic system of the time, resulting in the frequent arrest of its writers and editors. Police pressure was also put on *La Revue Blanche*, a paper which included among its contributors writers such as Zola, Verlaine and Léon Blum.

The Chat Noir is one of the most celebrated 19th-century French cabaret bars, where entertainments included shadow plays, poetry, singing. There was often a political edge to the content. The venue published a magazine which helped build the brand but also disseminated more radical politics and satire, as well as art and writing by various of the cabaret's regular customers.

Non-conformists were questioning society politically but culturally too; the tensions in French society surfaced in battles over the practice and purpose of art. Traditionally, the Académie des Beaux-Arts was the official arbiter of French art. Sanctioned by the Emperor, the Académie chose the works for the annual and prestigious Paris Salon, through the exigencies of a rigidly traditional admissions jury, which excluded the avant-garde and the adventurous.

In 1863, the jury refused what is now regarded as one of the great paintings of the 19th century, Édouard Manet's *Le Déjeuner sur l'herbe*. The work was criticised for its unrefined brush strokes – consciously applied and integral to Manet's desire to produce paintings that gave a sense of spontaneity – but serious outrage was reserved for Manet's depiction of nudity set, recognisably, in the Bois de Boulogne, a large public park situated to the west of Paris. French high society enjoyed riding in the park, which was also known for its widespread prostitution. The hypocrisy was huge. It was reckoned that in the Louvre at the time there were around fifty paintings showing various stages of nudity, but they were derived from ancient, historical or biblical themes. *Le Déjeuner sur l'herbe* placed carnality firmly in the contemporary world of the Parisian bourgeoisie.

From 1870, Manet was living close to Place Pigalle. Until his death in 1883, he painted many of the interiors and *terrasses* of his local bars, restaurants, and cabarets. Manet, it seemed, understood the precepts laid down by Charles Baudelaire in various articles in the newspaper *Le Figaro* during 1863. Baudelaire believed the modern artist should 'set up his [sic] house in the heart of the multitude, amid the ebb and flow of motion, in the midst of the fugitive and the infinite'.[4]

Protests eventually persuaded the Emperor's office to establish a second exhibition including work that had been refused by the Académie; this was dubbed the Salon des Refusés. Twenty years later, in 1884, those who didn't wish to conform to the rigidity of conservative taste organised themselves into the Société des Artistes Indépendants. As Édouard Manet put it: 'To exhibit is to find friends and allies for the struggle.'

On his arrival in Paris, then, Picasso had the good fortune to be plugged into an alternative away from the institutions; a growing network of artists,

---

[4] Marshall Berman, *All That Is Solid Melts into Air* (Verso, 1983), 145.

magazines, art dealers, and reviewers with a track record of challenging the mainstream and gaining a foothold for pioneering work. But while the radicals self-organised, reactionaries resistant to change looked to strengthen their power. In the years immediately after the Commune, the ultra-conservative Government of the Moral Order controlled the country, pushing back against any residual support for the Commune's ideals. The construction of Sacré Cœur at the top of the Montmartre hill – which started in 1875 – took on extra significance in the wake of the Commune, the authorities demolishing houses, and displacing the poor, before erecting a huge building reasserting the power of the priests and the existing hierarchy.

In his short story collection, *Black Spring*, Henry Miller describes Sacré Cœur as 'a dream embedded in stone' but Sacré Cœur remains controversial; it's not so much a dream as an assertion of power, a threat, a deliberately constructed reminder to the locals of where the real power resides.[5] 'This astonishing edifice mocks Paris even as it dominates her,' declared a writer in *Le Père Peinard* in 1897.[6]

---

[5] Miller is more characteristically irreverent with a further description of Sacré Cœur as 'the belly of a jaded woman'.
[6] *Le Père Peinard*, issue 47, 12 September 1897.

So many societies appear only able to function if the history or contemporary presence of underlying conflicts is unacknowledged. Tourists jostle on the steps of Sacré Cœur for the best photo, but Montmartre's history of subversion is buried. So too the status of the building itself, a monument to the battles between conformity and freedom, order and rebellion.

+

A young person's desire to immerse themselves in adventurous noisy late-night craziness is far from unusual. Even at forty years old, the American novelist Theodore Dreiser was thrilled by what he experienced during his first visit to Paris in 1913. Dreiser described a long night out in Montmartre and Pigalle which concluded with a visit to the upscale Abbaye de Thélème: 'the place was fairly vibrating with a wild desire to live'.[7]

Nightlife venues of Montmartre and Pigalle varied from deluxe clubs for rich tourists to dives alive with ideas, from kitchens serving rabbit stew to those serving lobster *à l'Américaine*, from solo pianists to gypsy troupes singing of wild nights and lost love.

---

[7] Theodore Dreiser, *A Traveler at Forty* (The Century Co., 1913), 220.

And artists, and anarchists, drunks, and ladies of the night; dancers, vagabonds and bandits; the beautiful and the damned.

The 1903 *Pleasure Guide to Paris for Bachelors* includes Dreiser's favourite venue, the Abbaye de Thélème. It's recommended, but not without a proviso or two: 'Women congregate here in great numbers from all parts of Paris, some of them being very doubtful characters; therefore it behoves the English visitor to be on his guard as to his purse and person.'[8]

The number of venues the *Guide* describes as 'low houses' or places where 'low women' are in attendance is considerable. Picasso was no stranger to such goings-on. When he was growing up in Malaga, his father – an artist and art teacher – had a Sunday ritual that included a visit to a brothel after attending Mass. Picasso lost his virginity at the age of thirteen or fourteen in one such place of business. In Paris, he developed a particular liking for a brothel on the rue de Londres, south of Pigalle and towards the Gare Saint-Lazare.

Police seldom intervened in such *maisons de tolérance* – the licensed brothels required to run under legally enforceable conditions, including regular physical inspection of the women working there to attempt

---

[8] Day, *Pleasure Guide*, 128.

to halt the spread of sexually transmitted diseases. At a night out at the Moulin de la Galette you could dance quadrilles and raucous polkas, and see and be seen, but you'd also be aware you were in the presence of prostitutes and their pimps, but, in addition, a degree of informal sex work too; poverty-stricken women, penniless mothers, low-paid servant girls and laundresses all looking to supplement their meagre wages.

Picasso and Henri de Toulouse-Lautrec never met (very ill, and knowing he'd never recover, Toulouse-Lautrec had left Paris before Picasso first visited, and died in 1901). His work was well known to Picasso, including the paintings in which Toulouse-Lautrec had extensively depicted life in the brothels of Pigalle and among the inmates of the Saint Lazare women's prison on rue du Faubourg-Saint-Denis (many of them sex workers). Picasso had an interest in the darker side of the *Belle Époque*; he followed Toulouse-Lautrec to the prison, painting there works like *Femme aux Bras Croisés*. This was Picasso's 'blue period', dating from the second half of 1901, just months after the death of Casagemas, when themes of poverty, loneliness, death and guilt washed through his work; his subjects included portraits of the destitute, and sick, his colour palette dominated by muted, murky shades of blue/grey.

+

The inhabitants of Paris develop a loyal and intimate relationship with their neighbourhood café bars. In a letter to his friend Félix Bracquemond in 1879, Degas writes that every single day ('with rare exceptions') he eats his lunch at the Café La Rochefoucauld on the corner of rue Notre-Dame de Lorette and rue Rochefoucauld.[9]

For customers, such cafés are a second home, a ritual, a place to pass the time, and, especially from the pavement *terrasse*, to watch the world go by. It's simple enough for a group of regulars to materialise. Dexys Midnight Runners hung out in 'greasy spoon' cafés on Broad Street in Birmingham in the late 1970s (like the Tow Rope, and Rendezvous) where they would practise the art of making a milky coffee last an hour, and discuss plans to change the world. They celebrated their version of café culture in 'The Teams That Meet in Caffs', an instrumental track on their debut album.

In Barcelona in 1899, Picasso had been a visitor to a modernist hangout, a café called Els Quatre Gats – which had been inspired by the Chat Noir in Paris – where food and drink was served, and music

---

[9] Richard Kendall (ed.), *Degas by Himself* (Little, Brown, 1987), 68.

performances, art exhibitions and literary discussions took place. The young Picasso was fascinated by the goings-on at Els Quatre Gats. There he met Ramon Casas and Santiago Rusiñol, two men who had lived in Montmartre at various times from the 1890s onwards, and became, in some senses, mentors for Picasso. It was perhaps inevitable that the young Picasso would find his way to Paris.

Artists of all nationalities were attracted to Paris. Van Gogh discovered a home-from-home at the Nouvelle Athènes on Place Pigalle. At the Nouvelle Athènes in the 1870s through to the 1880s, you might also have seen Manet, Degas, Cézanne, and Toulouse-Lautrec. Manet in particular encouraged regular meet-ups of like-minded artists at the Nouvelle Athènes, for creative sustenance and, no doubt, to plot against the Académie des Beaux-Arts. Manet believed that organising space at an exhibition was an important way to find friends and allies; for him, the same was true of café bars. Writer Roger Shattuck goes so far as to argue that 'The Café Guerbois and the Nouvelle Athènes in the sixties and seventies had nurtured the first artistic movement entirely organized in cafés: impressionism.'[10]

---

[10] Roger Shattuck, *The Banquet Years* (Vintage Books, 1968), 11.

That's the ever-present, ever-fertile power of the cell: a small group of disaffected outsiders creating a significant cultural moment, or a movement. The established institutions and the public at large might take fright at the unconventional goings-on but from weirdos in the cheap gathering spaces, ideas dismissed as new fads can knock culture into a new era.

Van Gogh's longest stay in Paris was two years from 1886, during which he painted *Café Table with Absinthe*. He was fond of absinthe – very much a favoured drink in that era. Van Gogh was drinking to excess; it wasn't doing much good for his physical or mental health. Venues like the Nouvelle Athènes would also offer breakfast, *menu du jour* in the middle of the day, and more ambitious fare in the restaurant area in the evening, but generally descend into a shouty riot of beer and brandy by the last and lost hours after midnight.

In 1900, the predominant music entertaining customers at the Nouvelle Athènes was a small Tzigane orchestra, six or seven musicians wearing red uniforms, playing a mix of violins and guitars. There wasn't a single or simple definition of what was meant by Tzigane music in Paris in this era, other than it being music that sounded like it had some 'gypsy' heritage (the word 'Tzigane' is derived from the generic

European term for 'gypsy'). The players were usually Romanian and Hungarian.

A Tzigane orchestra could conjure drama, emotion, or high spirits. Picasso was no doubt reminded of flamenco, a music culture associated with the Andalusian Roma of southern Spain that he'd known well in his young days and later in life became even more passionate about. In fact, Picasso claimed he didn't like much music beyond flamenco. He isn't the only person whose music taste barely changed after the age of eighteen.

In the early years of Picasso's time in Paris, he'd have heard singers entertaining listeners with songs of all kinds – comic, satirical, bawdy, sentimental – and unaccompanied pianists. In the years just prior to Picasso's arrival in the city, Erik Satie was among the pianists working in bars in Montmartre. In his early twenties, while he was employed at the Chat Noir, Satie combined a late-night bohemian lifestyle with composing some of his most celebrated pieces of music, including *Trois Gymnopédies* (1888). After he walked out on the Chat Noir in 1891, he began working at the nearby Auberge du Clou where he met and became a close friend of Claude Debussy.

The notion of what constituted 'performance' at these venues wasn't limited to what was onstage.

Inside and on the *terrasses*, the people-watching was addictive; the promenading, the mysterious passers-by, the theatre of it all, the characters, the fashion statements.

When Casagemas listed some of the bars and cabaret clubs he and Picasso had visited in a letter to friends, he mentioned a hell-themed restaurant and nightclub called L'Enfer. The front door on the boulevard de Clichy was designed to evoke entering hell through the jaws of the devil. In the depths of the venue, a small group of musicians played selections from works such as Charles Gounod's *Faust*, and smouldering fires sent thick smoke through the hellish underworld.

Curiosity was key to the creativity around Picasso in Paris; a creative flow of ideas. Artists, venue operators, dancers, musicians, writers, were promiscuous in their embrace of the unfamiliar; in one era everyone was turning Japanese. In 1887, Van Gogh had a brief relationship with Agostina Segatori, the owner of the Café du Tambourin (on boulevard de Clichy) and painted her portrait; part of his collection of Japanese prints can be seen in the background. Toulouse-Lautrec absorbed influences from Japanese art into his work and also designed posters for a nightclub called Le Divan Japonais on rue des Martyrs.

The club, incidentally, is still functioning as a dance hall, but now under the name Le Divan du Monde. Next door, and linked to it, is a small cabaret venue, Madame Arthur – historic and atmospheric – which pioneered drag shows in Paris.

Another example of this sense of restless adventure came after the Great War and through the 1920s when Black American jazz musicians brought new sounds and energy to the nightclubs in Montmartre and Pigalle. The Nouvelles Athènes had three floors: basement, ground floor, and first floor. In 1927, Ada 'Bricktop' Smith established her celebrated bar and jazz venue on the first floor, accessed via a doorway a little way down rue Pigalle (now named rue Jean-Baptiste Pigalle), and up a steep flight of stairs. Performers there included Josephine Baker and customers included the writer John Steinbeck.

By and through the mid 1960s, the former Nouvelles Athènes building operated as two strip clubs with the names Narcisse and Le Sphinx. In the late 1980s and 1990s, the first floor housed the New Moon, one of those small and unashamedly scuzzy venues every city should have; groups like Mano Negra, and Les Wampas, played there. Stiv Bators of the Dead Boys – regulars at the quintessential scuzzy rock venue, New York's CBGB – was living in Paris in 1987.

He performed at New Moon in March of that year alongside his buddy Johnny Thunders. The original building has since been demolished; in its place is a branch of the organic food chain Bio c'Bon – to date by far the most wholesome business on that site.

+

In 1903, on Place Pigalle and just yards from the Nouvelle Athènes, there was another all-day, late-night venue: the Rat Mort, where a Tzigane orchestra played until four in the morning. In addition to attracting a bohemian collection of artists, writers, and journalists, the Rat Mort was also the haunt of anarchists, dancers, and prostitutes, and – usually late in the evening – it was also a favourite of the lesbian community. A popular lesbian bar, Le Hanneton, was just a hundred yards down rue Pigalle.

Toulouse-Lautrec's painting *In a Private Booth at the Rat Mort* (1899) features a fancily dressed woman with a billowing wig and red lipstick sitting in front of a table of drinks, perhaps a relatively high-class prostitute who has just finished work or is taking a break late on in the night.[11] She's sitting slight-

---

[11] Art historians have identified the woman as a prostitute called Lucy Jourdain.

ly askew, with unfocused eyes, and another glass of champagne in her hand. The indoor, artificial light – particularly a glow from the lamp on the left – is throwing unpredictable shadows. The tableau is blurry, even hallucinatory; is it possible that it's the viewer looking at the subjects that's had a few too many drinks? A man is sharing the booth (a '*cabinet particulier*', a private space designed for intimate liaisons); he's so far to the edge of the painting, we don't see his profile or his features. He remains – as he no doubt wishes to be – anonymous. That smear of hot red lipstick on the woman's mouth is at the dead centre of the painting.

Paris at night was transformed as gas lighting and then electricity replaced oil lamps through and after the last decades of the 19th century. In the rain, at dusk, in the dark, shop windows were enticingly bright, cafés were warm little luminous dream palaces. The aesthetic of the city after dark was transformed. Rather than looking at traditional subjects – an aristocrat and his family, a beach, or a sunlit glade – painters of all kinds were captivated by urban scenes, and the atmospheric effects of street lights and coloured bulbs in bars. In Luigi Loir's *Carousel de la Porte Dorée* (1870) the electric light bulbs of the carousel stand out luridly brightly in a grey Paris evening. In *Paris at*

Night (1889) by Charles Courtney Curran, yellowish gas lights illuminate the scene, their reflections glittering on the wet pavements.

The popularity of cabarets and bars was increasing partly as a result of the safety promised by better-lit streets and venues, and partly by the extra spending power and leisure time enjoyed by the bourgeoisie during *La Belle Époque*. The working class and the bourgeoisie intermingled in a way unlike in daylight hours. Some historically working-class areas and venues experienced a form of gentrification as relatively upscale venues started appearing in run-down areas. There was disgust among locals when the arrival of throngs of American tourists early in the 1900s pushed up food and drink prices.

Other innovations in the night-life industry during the second half of the 19th century included a move away from male-only waiting staff in cafés. The employment of waitresses, however, was a practical change to do with staffing levels, rather than a sign of female liberation; the number of café bars in Paris jumped from 4,000 in 1851 to 42,000 in 1885.

In Manet's painting *Corner of a Café Concert* (1878), a waitress takes centre stage. The painting went through several different versions until, finally, Manet eschewed anything remotely like a panoramic view, instead providing a cropped snapshot of the waitress at work. Capturing a sense of the hectic action in the bar, Manet is dialling up the sense of spontaneity. We're reminded of Baudelaire's plea for modern artists to portray 'the eternal and the immutable' and focus on 'the fugitive, the contingent'.

+

Picasso's first painting in his Paris years portrayed the interior of the dance hall at the Moulin de la Galette, dating from around November 1900. It was included in his debut exhibition in Paris in June 1901 at a gallery run by Ambroise Vollard. The critic Gustave Coquiot, who helped promote the show, described Picasso as 'an artist who paints round the clock, who never believes the day is over, in a city that offers a different spectacle every minute'.[12]

Most of the work exhibited revealed the painter's major influences, including the use of colour from Cézanne, the effect of capturing a fleeting moment from Manet's rapid brush strokes, and a heavy dose of Toulouse-Lautrec, who had painted the goings-on in the Moulin de la Galette several times in the 1880s.

---

[12] Barnaby Wright (ed.), *Becoming Picasso: Paris 1901* (Courtauld Gallery, 2013), 23.

The exhibition included several other paintings of nightlife, cafés, cabaret bars, and sex workers,
including one entitled *French Can-can*, which played
up the titillating aspect of the dance; the accent on a
flurry of white petticoats, flashes of black stocking,
and eye-catching red garters rather than the faces of
the women.

During and after the exhibition at Ambroise
Vollard's gallery, artists and (particularly) writers and
others involved in the cultural scene in Paris began
to befriend Picasso, widening his circle; Max Jacob,
an eccentric gay man who wrote obscure poetry, and
painted rather unsuccessfully, became one of Picasso's
closest friends and supporters.

Picasso received commissions for the kind
of work Toulouse-Lautrec had pioneered, including
a poster advertising a pop-up outdoor venue run by
the Moulin Rouge near the Champs Élysées during
the summer. He also contributed drawings of cabaret
performers to a magazine called *Frou-Frou*; the work
wasn't challenging but it paid the bills.

Even in the youthful paintings collected in the
exhibition at Galerie Vollard, the world of hardship is
present. The painting *A Montmartre Café* – executed
on the edge of Picasso's introspective and melancholic 'blue period' – depicts an interior, with two tables

of single diners. Outside, the colours are murky grey, brown; it could be raining. Inside is more colourful but not much more cheerful. A flower seller dressed in black with a child at her side is waiting for one of the diners to look up from her soup and maybe buy something. Is Picasso more interested in the plight of the destitute than the diners? To the right, a mother holds her swaddled baby to her, her proud eyes looking directly out of the painting, imploringly.

Picasso's work in this first exhibition had depth and some daring elements but wasn't by any means as adventurous as his paintings would be five or six years later; but he needed a foothold in the Paris art market and, like every young artist, he was still working his way through his influences to find an individual vision. Already, however, the distance between his vision and that of the impressionist Pierre-Auguste Renoir was clear. Renoir's is the most well-known 19th-century painting of the Moulin de la Galette; a view of the outdoor space painted in 1876. Renoir gives a lush rendering of the scene, shot through with good taste and a sense of temperance. Fresh-faced *Belle Époque* girls, jolly folk with parasols, young friends gathered for some civilised socialising on a summer evening.

Picasso's painting is set inside the Moulin de le Galette, and after dark. The character of the pro-

ceedings would have been very different; late nights
in Montmartre are generally and historically suffused
with more erotic thrill, a chance to revel in intoxica-
tion and transgression.

It's possible that when Renoir had set up his
easel *en plein air* in 1876 the crowd he saw included no drunks, no pimps, no sleaze. But in any case,
Renoir's attitude to art would have held him back from
searching out and representing the underworld that
intrigued Toulouse-Lautrec and Picasso. According to
David Sweetman, the painting springs from 'the notion that art should be a begetter of wellbeing and joy,
rather than a vehicle for portraying the truth about
contemporary life that Baudelaire had proposed'.[13]

Picasso's depiction of the Moulin de la Galette
is very different to Renoir's; the colour palette is lurid;
couples are tight together; sinister and predatory men
at the back survey the dance floor; and there's a hint
of lesbianism in the foreground, and a very knowing
look from the women staring straight at the viewer
from the lower left of the painting.

Out late in Pigalle, Dreiser discovered a 'wild
desire to live', aware that what he was sensing wasn't

---

[13] David Sweetman, *Toulouse-Lautrec and the Fin-de-siecle* (Hodder & Stoughton,
1993), 79-80.

pure or pretty. Unstable or shady characters were never far away. Pursuing the wild desire to live – bliss descending, nerves jangling – involves acknowledging the proximity of chaos to glitter.

+

On his fourth visit to Paris, in 1904, Picasso took up permanent residence in the city, taking a room at the Bateau-Lavoir halfway up the Montmartre hill on Place Émile Goudeau. The years there were crucial in his development as an artist, and were mostly spent living a genuinely bohemian existence with Fernande Olivier; writer Dan Franck calls her 'his great love'.[14]

The Bateau-Lavoir was an ex-piano factory, a wooden building that had then been converted into very basic, cramped and ramshackle accommodation. Fernande, who earned a very modest living as an artist's model, had been living at the Bateau-Lavoir with her lover Laurent Debienne since the autumn of 1900. Fernande was inspired by the creative environment at the Bateau-Lavoir and began also to paint.

Fernande and Picasso caught glimpses of each other in the course of their daily lives. Fernande

---

[14] Dan Franck, *Bohemian Paris* (Grove Press, 2001), 56.

later recalled her first impressions of the artist, that Picasso was 'small and worried-looking'.[15] Elsewhere, she described how he was brooding with a 'suppressed fire' and 'an intense gaze'.

Among the transient and often artistic residents of the Bateau-Lavoir were Dutch artist Kees van Dongen and his family, Amadeo Modigliani, Juan Gris, André Salmon, Pierre Mac Orlan, and Marie Laurencin. It became a wider friendship group that also included André Derain, Henri Rousseau, Guillaume Apollinaire, and Alfred Jarry. Many of them had periods of extreme poverty, including the painter Rousseau. When Rousseau died in September 1910, he was laid to rest in a pauper's grave in the Bagneux cemetery.[16]

If Sacré Cœur represented one side of the battle between order and freedom, the Bateau-Lavoir represented the other. Alfred Jarry already had a legendary reputation among the avant-garde after the staging of his *Ubu Roi*, a play so disruptive and uncompromised and challenging to order, authority and French hierarchies, that the theatre crowd rioted at its 1896 premiere, which, in the face of such hostility, turned out also to be its closing night.

---

[15] Film documentary shown at Musée de Montmartre, November 2022.
[16] Shattuck, *Banquet Years*, 76.

Artists and writers associated with the Bateau-Lavoir often had lifestyles as scandalous as their art. The café-hotel Bouscarat on rue Norvins had a reputation for attracting the best-looking dancers from the Moulin Rouge; it was also where Picasso and his circle often sourced their opium. There were also opium dens hidden away in Montmartre and Pigalle, including one on rue de Douai run by George Braque's mistress Paulette Philippi which also functioned as a brothel. One of her guests, Jean Mollet – Apollinaire and Cocteau nicknamed him 'the Baron' – is said to have been the person who introduced Picasso to opium. The Baron would arrive at Paulette's with a basket of oysters and two litres of mêlé-cassis, and sometimes stay one day, sometimes, by accident, eight or nine days.

By 1906, Picasso was smoking opium several times a week although he never considered the drug as a creative tool for his work. It was a means to escape, and often, specifically, a means to escape with Fernande. She had suffered several traumatic relationships and sexual brutality and discovered that opium helped soothe her mind, albeit temporarily, enabling her to enjoy her intimate time with Picasso. Later in life she declared: 'It's probably thanks to opium that

I've discovered the true meaning of the word love'.[17]

Picasso's positivity about opium waned in 1908 when Karl-Heinz Wiegels, a young German painter he had befriended, suffered a psychotic episode after bingeing on opium, hashish, and ether; Picasso found him hanging from a ceiling beam in the Bateau-Lavoir.

Sister and brother Gertrude and Leo Stein were among the first art collectors to take an interest in Picasso's paintings. In 1905, the American siblings began travelling from their apartment on rue de Fleurus in Montparnasse, across Paris to the Bateau-Lavoir to visit Picasso. Gertrude Stein enjoyed the company of many of his friends, including Apollinaire, describing him as 'very attractive and interesting. He had a head like one of the late roman emperors'.[18]

By all accounts, Apollinaire was a charming, talkative man with a lot of creative energy. He wrote in *La Revue Blanche* and, with friends, founded other small magazines. Alcohol was his drug of choice, although by the beginning of 1914 he was smoking opium most weeks with the painter Francis Pica-

---

[17] Fernande Olivier quoted in Amy Licence, *Bohemian Lives* (Amberley Publishing, 2019), 114.
[18] Gertrude Stein, *The Autobiography of Alice B. Toklas* (Penguin, 1966), 66.

bia. His 155-line poem 'Zone' (1913) is both radical and mesmerising, a collage of under-punctuated thoughts, digressions, and descriptions tracking a walk through Paris from sunrise one day until daylight arrives the next day and 'like a dark beauty night withdraws'.[19]

Picasso, Apollinaire, the writer and journalist André Salmon, and the gay poet Max Jacob were a close-knit group of night-out buddies. Salmon later described visits to a bar called Fauvet on Place des Abbesses, recalling 'poets and painters fraternised with vagrants'. At Fauvet, Picasso and his friends would drink cheap red wine or *mominette* (a small glass of imitation or bootlegged absinthe). The bar featured an exciting modern development: a coin-operated electric organ.

Like most citizens of Paris, Picasso and Fernande spent most of their time in their local neighbourhood, but they would cross the city, over the river, to visit the Steins. On quiet Tuesdays, Picasso and Fernande took to walking across the river to a bar called Café de Flore to meet Salmon and Apollinaire; Apollinaire used the café as an informal office for his periodical *Les Soirées de Paris*. Fernande recalled fre-

---

[19] Translation by Samuel Beckett.

netic and inspiring conversations with Apollinaire, especially after one particular night in a bar: 'What discussions! What madness! We left only when the owner threw us out into the street'.

Many of Picasso's comrades were bold and iconoclastic – I'm thinking particularly of Jarry, Apollinaire, and Satie. In one of Apollinaire's later poems, 'La Jolie Russes' (1918), he champions the non-conformists 'always fighting at the frontiers / Of the limitless and the future'. Disruption by the avant-garde is not unreasonable, he goes on to explain; its fruits are new ways of escaping the cage, seeing new horizons, new ways of living. 'We want to give you vast and strange territories... colours never seen before,' he says. He's talking about art like it's a night out, an experience of ravenously seeking highs and inspiration. He's celebrating the curious, the misfits; '*Nous qui quêtons partout l'aventure,*' he says ('We who seek adventure everywhere').

+

Louis Fernando had established a circus in the Loire region of France before creating another on a large site at the corner of the boulevard de Rochechouart and the rue des Martyrs. It's now hard to imagine a circus in the midst of shops, houses, and bars but in the area at the very edge of the boundaries of the city of Paris in 1875 undeveloped sites were plentiful. The location made perfect sense; a working-class neighbourhood which was already a centre of popular entertainment. Soon enough, the sights, the colour, the excitements of the circus, also attracted the attention of many of the artists living locally.

When Cirque Fernando hit financial troubles, the enterprise was taken over by one of the most popular clowns of the era, Geronimo 'Boum-Boum' Medrano and given the name Cirque Medrano. The Medrano clowns began to forsake traditional clown costumes and dress instead in baggy suits and other ill-fitting clothes, a look later well-known on Charlie Chaplin. In 1947, one of the great silent clowns, Buster Keaton, performed at the Cirque Medrano when he was resurrecting his career; Chico Marx flew from America to join the audience.[20]

Picasso and Fernande would visit the Medrano with friends three or even four times a week. According to Fernande, she never saw Picasso laugh so genuinely as he did when he was at the circus ('*Ce*

---

[20] Film of Buster Keaton at the Cirque Medrano (https://youtu.be/2DirzpKp6ww).

fait une révélation, she wrote).[21] Harlequins, acrobats, and other performers entertained Picasso, but in addition, their itinerant lifestyle, and existence outside traditional society, fascinated him (with Fernande, he'd go drinking with many of the circus people at the Café de la Place Blanche).

Picasso often depicted himself as a harlequin, not just in the Lapin Agile painting but on dozens of other occasions too. Perhaps he related to their outsider status or, as a painter, to their endeavours to express emotion without words. Or was it deeper than that? Picasso's 1905 painting *Family of Saltimbanques* depicts a family of acrobats wandering in a featureless landscape, rendered in subdued tones, including a pale rose, and a washed-out brown. His love life, where he lived, the styles he worked in, the places where he drank, the loyalties of art critics: there was a good deal Picasso may have felt was temporary, transient, provisional. The circus performers were entertainers, and misfits. Their peripatetic life looked like a kind of freedom, but they had no place called home. He reacted with joy to their work, but Picasso saw the tears of a clown in their lives too.

---

[21] Schlesser, *Picasso À Paris*, 37.

+

Irish writer George Moore journeyed to Paris many times, carrying with him a passionate enthusiasm for the work of novelist Émile Zola; the two became friends. Moore was also a friend and admirer of Édouard Manet. In an unfinished portrait of 1878 or 1879, Manet depicts the Irishman at the café Nouvelle Athènes.

Moore loved the Nouvelle Athènes and writes some beautiful pages in his 1886 memoir *Confessions of a Young Man* about falling out of the venue in the early hours of the morning. Elsewhere, he called it 'the ideal café', and explained the importance of café culture: 'In the Middle Ages, young men went in search of the Grail,' he wrote. 'Today the café is the quest of a young man in search of artistic education.'[22]

His words accurately reflect the status of the Montmartre cafés but inadvertently also reveal an uncomfortable truth. That it was a man's world. Sadly, of course, this wasn't true only of Paris or only of that era, but generally a single woman was viewed with suspicion in cafés, bars, and nightclubs. Invariably the

---

[22] George Moore, 'Reminiscences of the Impressionist Painters', published in *Scribner's Magazine*, vol. 39 (1906), 196.

assumption would be that she was a sex worker. The presence of women in the painting caused controversies around Ilya Repin's large canvas work *Paris Café* (1875); critics and audiences were unsettled by the sense of sexual chemistry in the air and by the stares of the men at a scene-stealing woman at the very front of the café bar.

The notion of women as equals was rarely accepted in artistic and intellectual circles. Fortunately, to a degree this would change by the mid 1930s, with the conspicuous contribution made by women to Surrealism, and by the end of the 19th century there were already some stirrings of change in the art schools. In 1894, Suzanne Valadon became the first woman to be admitted to the Société Nationale des Beaux-Arts, and the number of female students at the Sorbonne doubled between 1897 and 1906 (although male students still comprised 75 per cent of the university).

In a culture that reeked of misogyny, it would be heartening to report that Picasso was one of the enlightened few, but it wasn't so. Most of his female or male relationships were about power; he wanted to be adored. Whatever dreams or talents the women in his gaze may have had, Picasso would habitually view them as his muse, mistress, property, prey. His ceaseless infidelity, and his attitudes towards his prey – sequentially, from attraction to obsession to contempt – were lifelong patterns of behaviour.

Picasso would replace Fernande with Eva Gouel. Owing to Eva's deteriorating health during the first winter of the Great War, she was hospitalised in a clinic several miles away. Seemingly unable to spend time without a woman in his bed, Picasso began an affair with a neighbour, Gaby Lespinasse. He visited Eva most days, and most nights he betrayed her. Eva died in December 1915.

Much later, in 1927, Picasso met Marie-Thérèse Walter when she was seventeen years old, thirty years his junior. His power over her was dazzling and destructive, their sex life full of sadistic violence. 'I always cried with Pablo Picasso,' Marie-Thérèse told writer Pierre Cabanne in 1974. 'I bowed my head in front of him.'

Going right back to the Bateau-Lavoir, especially at the beginning of their relationship, Picasso would forbid Fernande from leaving home unaccompanied, even to go shopping. He'd convinced himself that she'd not be able to resist the many men who he believed would proposition her outside the grocery store.

In 1909, with Picasso's earnings increasing, he and Fernande left the Bateau-Lavoir for an apartment at 11, boulevard de Clichy. The move wasn't far geographically, but in other ways it was a long way from the deprivations of the Bateau-Lavoir. The couple acquired a purple velvet Louis Philippe sofa and the services of a maid. Gertrude Stein noted that the apartment had lots of sunshine, so much room, and the maid served very decent soufflés, but things didn't seem well with Fernande. Stein reported: 'On the whole however Fernande was not quite as happy as she had been'.[23]

Picasso had short-lived affairs with numerous young women in these years, but even when he was seeing someone seriously or for any length of time (someone who he felt he could make a home with, perhaps) he never had the compassion or the courage to end a relationship. Well before a final break, Picasso would begin to prioritise someone new.

Once living in the new apartment, Fernande and Picasso took to meeting Polish painter Louis Marcoussis and his girlfriend Marcelle Humbert, at a neighbourhood bar called L'Ermitage. Sometimes the four of them would be invited over to rue de Fleurus to see the Steins. Picasso began to prise Marcelle away and instigate an affair; he also persuaded her to return to her birthname Eva Gouel.

---

[23] Stein, *Alice B. Toklas*, 121.

Eva inspired the Cubist work *Woman with a Guitar* (1912). Six strings in the centre of the painting signify the presence of a guitar, but there's nothing instantly recognisable in the work. It's almost the essence of Cubism: presenting a fractured image composed of lines forming into angles; multiple planes and shadings; and a colour palette limited to muddy cream going into sludgy brown, and slate grey. '*Ma Jolie*' ('my pretty one') is inscribed on the painting. This is a refrain from a popular French cabaret song, except those who knew how Picasso's mind and art operated knew there were questions to be asked. Gertrude Stein realised something was up: 'Fernande is certainly not my jolie, I wonder who it is?' she said.[24]

In October 1911, a group of Italian Futurists led by Filippo Marinetti journeyed to Paris to progress an idea for an exhibition in France. They were in touch with Picasso and Fernande, hoping to pay a visit to Picasso. Fernande met several of the Italians in L'Ermitage, including a twenty-three-year-old artist from Vicenza in Northern Italy called Ubaldo Oppi. Fernande and Oppi embarked on an affair, word soon reaching Picasso. He wrote to Braque: 'Fernande has ditched me for a Futurist...'

[24] Stein, *Alice B. Toklas*, 122.

His relationship with Fernande finally at an
end, Picasso left Montmartre after twelve years in the
area. With Eva, he moved across the river to Montparnasse, eventually settling at 5 bis rue Schoelcher,
a luxurious building on a quiet street. Picasso's studio
had natural light from a huge bay window.

+

The extraordinary power of avant-garde art in Paris
in the first decades of the 20th century included wild
experiments in the world of ballet, which, perhaps in-
evitably, triggered hostility. Conservative voices had
kept themselves busy decrying paintings, newspapers,
poems, and now radical ideas at the ballet drew their
attention.

Key to this was the founding in the city of the
dance company Ballets Russes by the impresario Ser-
gei Diaghilev, and the subsequent involvement of the
likes of Vaslav Nijinsky, Igor Stravinsky, Jean Cocteau,
and, via the latter, Picasso and Erik Satie.

In May 1912, at the premiere of the ballet
L'Après-midi d'un faune, sections of the audience
were scandalised by the sexually explicit choreog-
raphy by Nijinsky. The following year, Le Sacre du
printemps caused uproar; the French newspaper Le

Figaro declared that the ballet was 'a laborious and puerile barbarity'.

In the same years, Georges Braque and Picasso were detonating the explosive shock of the Cubist movement. Braque lived on rue d'Orsel on the eastern edge of *la Butte*, close to where the Théâtre de l'Atelier can now be found. Picasso was aware of work of Braque's like the paintings of trees and houses at l'Estaque (1908), a maelstrom of muted colours, lines, shapes, almost abstract images, certainly prefiguring Cubism.

Picasso and Braque challenged and encouraged each other (in Braque's words, the two 'were like mountain-climbers roped together'). Braque began incorporating small strips of mass-produced faux bois wallpaper into charcoal drawings, and Picasso created the art world's first collages, adding cut-up newspapers to his paintings. The first scrap of newsprint Picasso used in his collages was a piece of the Paris newspaper *Le Journal* he pasted into a work called *Guitar, Sheet Music and Glass* in 1912. 'LA BATAILLE S'EST ENGAGE[E]', the headline reads.

Whether the phrase – 'the battle has begun' – is a reference to current affairs or to the challenge to prevailing taste this new form of expression of Picasso's represented (or both: ambiguity abounds in his work), Picasso's continuing use of phrases in newspapers was a radical move – pioneering collage as an art form – with the effect of positioning personal feeling and the shared world into the same frame.

A specific attraction of the guitar for Picasso was its curves, and the sound hole, which gave him opportunities to connect the instrument to the female form. Guitars, violins, sheet music, bottles, wine glasses, carafes, and other objects associated with the world of drink, cafés, and nightlife proliferated in his work, before, during, after Cubism. I took some delight in discovering that the ground floor of the apartment on boulevard de Clichy that Fernande and Picasso occupied is now a shop selling and servicing electric guitars.

In another demonstration of his inventiveness, and his desire to see the world and represent everything in it in new ways, Picasso began creating 3D models of guitars, using materials including paper, string, painted wire and old cardboard boxes; a quirky and adventurous format which, again, was without precedent in the art world. It was also fragile in the extreme: the assemblage *Bar Table With Guitar* from 1913 is held together with nothing more than pins.

In April 1914, Picasso created a series of six small sculptures of an absinthe glass. They're a combination of artistic creation and a real everyday object; Picasso incorporated an actual piece of cutlery – a trowel-shaped, serrated spoon which absinthe drinkers would use to hold a sugar cube over a glass when preparing the drink. The sugar cube and the rest of the work is bronze; the six sculptures were made using the same cast but each is painted differently.

The glory of the idea, other than the introduction of the spoon, is the subject matter. Instead of taking on a subject traditionally categorised as appropriate for sculpture – young maidens, allegorical figures, busts of great men, characters from myth and history – Picasso has chosen something characteristic of Parisian nightlife but considered mundane, and transformed it into an art object. It was fifty years, but just a short step, to Andy Warhol's *Campbell's Soup Cans* painting.

+

At the outset of the Great War in 1914, Braque and André Salmon enlisted immediately. Apollinaire had been born in Rome to a Polish-Lithuanian mother and an unknown father who is thought to be an aristocrat from central Europe. As a child he spoke Polish, Italian and French; in his late teens he relocated to Paris and began calling himself Guillaume Apollinaire. Despite not being a French citizen, Apollinaire volunteered to fight for France in the war.

In 1914, Picasso was thirty-three years old,
watching friends leave for the trenches, and finding
many of his favourite venues were shut. Even back in
Pigalle, clubs closed their doors; many patrons and
staff members were called up to the army; and Paris
life during wartime included debilitating restrictions
on cafés (curfew at 8 p.m.) and restaurants (9.30 p.m.).
As Gertrude Stein later wrote, 'In the spring and early
summer of nineteen-fourteen the old life was over.'[25]

In Montmartre, Picasso had shared long and
chaotic nights out with friends almost as a matter of
course. He was older now, and the wartime lockdown
served to confirm that big nights out were behind
him. By the early 1920s, deeply embedded in a social-
ite life, he was no longer a young man, carefree and
anonymous. His daytime café habits were still important to him, but his nightlife usually revolved around
VIP events, and glittering parties.

In Picasso's new neighbourhood in Montparnasse, one bar that remained open during the war was
Café de la Rotonde. He'd visit alone sometimes, shuf-
fling into a back room, but he'd also be there when
he had company (his companion would often be the
model Pâquerette). In a photograph taken by Jean

----

[25] Stein, *Alice B. Toklas*, 155.

Cocteau, Picasso is outside La Rotonde with André Salmon and Amedeo Modigliani. La Rotonde wasn't particularly chic (Cocteau found it a little unrefined for his tastes), but it definitely didn't have the insalubrious qualities of the likes of the Lapin Agile. Some of the artists would covet the cutlery and crockery, finding it hard to resist taking items home. According to one account: 'At a party in his studio, an embarrassed Modigliani once served dinner to the café's owner with dishes and silverware pilfered from the restaurant.'[26]

It was through Jean Cocteau that Picasso became involved in the Ballets Russes. Cocteau was a keen supporter of Serge Diaghilev's activities in Paris. For the 1917 season of the Ballets Russes, Cocteau wrote a one-act scenario, invited Picasso to design the stage and set design, and the costumes, and Erik Satie to provide the music. The resultant work, *Parade*, was premiered on 18 May 1917. Satie's score – which included the unconventional sounds of engines, gunfire, and typewriters – was a major challenge to established taste. He also incorporated ragtime, café chansons, and dance hall melodies; modernism was bringing sounds born in run-down and working-class venues into previously rigidly conventional art spaces.

---

[26] Ellen Williams, *Picasso's Paris* (The Little Bookroom, 1999), 87.

The Great War ended any momentum in the evolution of Cubism, and the creative collaboration between Picasso and Braque finished. As was his restless way, Picasso was already moving on to other things, while Braque – who survived the war despite being seriously injured – returned to his painting with a renewed belief in colour and emotion more akin to the work of Matisse than Picasso. Picasso never had the chance to rekindle his friendship with Guillaume Apollinaire. In November 1918, Apollinaire died of Spanish flu, having also sustained serious head injuries in battle.

+

By the time of the premiere of *Parade*, Picasso had met Olga Khokhlova, a Russian ballet dancer; they married in July 1918, living together first in room 143 of the Hotel Lutetia and then at 23 rue La Boétie (rented for him and paid for by art dealer Paul Rosenberg). They were now in the 8th *arrondissement*, a quiet, well-off neighbourhood featuring opportunities for luxury shopping, and home to the Champs-Élysées and government buildings including the Élysée Palace.

From the end of 1921, Picasso took to frequenting Le Bœuf sur le Toit, a cabaret bar on the rue

Boissy d'Anglas about four streets away from rue de La Boétie, which attracted big names in fashion and the monied art brigade. It was all very jet set. At Le Bœuf sur le Toit, Picasso was mixing with a clientele including characters from the English upper class (among them the Prince of Wales), Spanish princes, diplomats, wealthy Americans, Coco Chanel, Jean Cocteau, and Nancy Cunard. They weren't the bohemians of the Lapin Agile; this was the aristocracy of the avant-garde.

At Le Bœuf sur le Toit art decorated the walls, including Francis Picabia's painting *L'Œil cacodylate* (now at the Centre Pompidou). Jazz groups had become the usual soundtrack to nights out where the beau monde gathered; the same was true in London, where customers at the upmarket Ciro's nightclub were entertained by jazz musicians.

Picasso enjoyed portraying musicians and dancers, as he does in a 1925 work entitled *Three Dancers*, although 'enjoyed' might not be quite the right word here. In fact, even 'dancers' seems wrong. In the violent orgy of contorted shapes, the three people morph into musicians also: a guitar player, a pianist, a jazz trio, a lethal *ménage à trois*. The colourful hedonistic abandon looks to have turned destructive. Faces grimace. There's blue sky through the window behind, but do the balcony rails turn into prison bars? I'm imagining Picasso hearing a jazz group at Le Bœuf sur le Toit and capturing what to a flamenco fan might seem like a harsh cacophony and then, in the painting, boosting and twisting its fierceness for tragic effect.

From 1931, chauffeur Marcel Boudia drove Picasso around in a luxury Hispano-Suiza, although one of his most frequent journeys was a short walk – while married and living with Olga, he'd set up Marie-Thérèse in an apartment in the same street, rue de La Boétie. Olga remained oblivious to the situation but she left him in 1935 when she discovered Marie-Thérèse had given birth to Picasso's child, a daughter, Maya.

Early in 1936, Picasso met Dora Maar. This time his strategy was to be open rather than clandestine; each woman was aware of the other. Dora Maar became Picasso's model, mistress and muse; in fact, she was all those things but so much more. Maar was an innovative photographer – a reputation she had gained prior to meeting Picasso – and had become a committed left-wing activist and a regular in the Place Blanche cafés that served as unofficial Surrealism HQs: the Café de la Place Blanche and the Cyrano, on the opposite side of the square (on the corner of rue Lepic).

Surrealism was blessed with several other young women with talent across various disciplines; foremost among them, Lee Miller. Others included Rogi André whose work includes several striking photographs of Jacqueline Lamba when Lamba was a performer at the Coliseum at 65 rue Rochechouart (her performances included swimming naked in a giant aquarium). Lamba studied at the École des Beaux-Arts, became a painter in her own right, married André Breton, and later became great friends with Frida Kahlo.[27]

After Dora Maar met Picasso, they were lovers for nine years. As well as pursuing her own work – her photographs of objects tended to be poetic, intriguing, unsettling even – she took pictures of Picasso's painting *Guernica* in his studio at the Grands Augustins, tracking its evolution.

Guernica is a breathtaking work, a wake-up call, a century-defining portrayal of violence. Picasso's restless exploration led to his work at any particular time showing signs of several styles, and the year he produced *Guernica* was no different. His *Weeping*

---

[27] Breton's fascinating book *L'Amour fou* is a celebration of his 'mad love' for Lamba, including descriptions of their first encounter, walking through the city in the 'marvellous rush of evening'.

Woman is based on an image in *Guernica* but melds the grim, grey and black palette of the larger painting into a colourful portrayal of a woman in a fine hat sitting in a bar (the figure, incidentally, is based on Dora Maar). The effect is to bring the grief of *Guernica* into a setting closer to home: everyday experience meets the shock of the news.

In another 1937 painting, *Cat Catching a Bird*, the cat and the bird are both rendered in a cartoon-like style, with the cat emblazoned in gloriously bright colours. It's not a cute painting though; it's uncomfortable. The cat killing the bird isn't just an illustration of violence but perhaps also some kind of confession or message on Picasso's part. It's as if the cat is Picasso, or representative somehow of a killer creative instinct; she appears to be pregnant – itself an act of creation – trapping and feeding off her prey. In addition, the cat has mismatched eyes – one open, one closed. The position of an artist involves being aware of, and, if necessary, feeding off, the exterior world, whilst also being able to look within themselves in a quest for personal insight.

This is not unlike the status of a café, between interior and exterior worlds. A place to draw upon the disciplines and introspection of solitary time – alone, perhaps at the back of the café, hunched over a notebook or sketchbook – but also taking in a view out, through a window or a doorway, or sitting on the *terrasse*, accessing the maelstrom of daily life.

During the Second World War, Paris suffered major shortages of food, amongst other deprivations. Picasso spent the first year of the war away from the capital. When he returned, he made some forays to Café de Flore, and a café restaurant called Le Catalan became his regular lunchtime spot; it was just a few doors along from the apartment he lived at with Dora Maar. Le Catalan appears to have been heavily reliant on black-market supplies (its semi-legal status underlined by the fact there was no sign outside). In 1943, he painted *Le buffet du 'Catalan'*, a still life of some of the food laid out on the sideboard. It's a luxuriant portrayal, a sign of the value to Picasso of simple pleasures during wartime. A chance to eat cherries and socialise.

Picasso's companions at Le Catalan included Paul Éluard, Léon-Paul Fargue, and Jacques Prévert. He'd go there with Dora Maar, although the venue was also where he met his next long-term lover, Françoise Gilot, forty years his junior. Dora Maar moved on, ill with the cruelty of it all. In 1947, Picasso left Paris, relocating to the South of France with Françoise Gilot; during their ten years together, they had two children, Claude and Paloma. Technically, throughout this time, he was still married to Olga Khokhlova.

Picasso died in 1973. At least one of his biographers sees a cry of anguish in his final self-portrait, from June the previous year. He was lost and had gone out of his way to alienate himself from his four children. He had destroyed lives, including his own. His eyes were dimmed, his magnetism neutered, although until the end he was adding to his extraordinary body of work.

Biographer John Richardson, friend of Picasso and author of a four-volume biography of the artist, concluded that Picasso had the propensity to be both tender and cruel, counselling, 'Whatever you say about Picasso, the reverse is also apt to be true. In life, as in art, he could be one of the kindest and one of the unkindest people I have ever known.'[28]

Dora Maar was less circumspect. One evening in 1945, she was driven to tell him this: 'As an artist you may be extraordinary, but morally speaking you're worthless.'[29] Posthumously, Maar's own work and that of other women artists in the past has been given over-

---

[28] Richardson interviewed by Jasper Rees, 2019 (https://theartsdesk.com/visual-arts/encounter-john-richardson-picassos-biographer-who-has-died-95).
[29] Arianna Stassinopoulos Huffington, *Picasso: Creator and Destroyer* (Simon & Schuster, 1988), 299.

due recognition. In 2019, Centre Pompidou Paris displayed hundreds of her photographs, photomontages, self-portraits, and paintings in a major exhibition. In one headline Dora Maar was described as 'a great photographer hidden behind the master of painting'.[30]

The life of Fernande Olivier has been celebrated at the Musée Montmartre at an exhibition which ended in February 2023. She was being given a voice, literally; the show included fascinating film clips of her talking about life in the Bateau-Lavoir.

The Beat poet Allen Ginsberg's 1959 poem 'At Apollinaire's Grave' is a homage to, but also a conjuring-up of, the spirit of the dead Frenchman. The Beats were drawn to him and Paris, basing themselves in a dirt-cheap ruin of a hotel on rue Gît-le-Cœur – just a few streets from Le Catalan and, a little further along, Café de Flore where Apollinaire worked on his magazine. Gregory Corso introduced Ginsberg to the place; Corso stayed for a long period in an attic room where he wrote the mushroom-cloud-shaped poem 'Bomb'. William Burroughs completed the final pages of *Naked Lunch* in the hotel bar.

---

[30] Amparo Serrano de Haro writing in theconversation.com
(https://theconversation.com/dora-maar-a-great-photographer-hidden-behind-the-master-of-painting-197101).

Every generation comes to identify its version of the Bateau-Lavoir years, the years of hunger and creativity, courage and daring. Every generation makes its own culture, finds its own cafés, pubs, clubs, coffee bars, greasy spoons, cheap gathering spaces, and takes on the world armed with fervent iconoclasm, and desperate for new forms of expression; though sometimes also with one eye on what the past can offer as ammunition for revolutions to come.

+

The lesbian hangout Le Hanneton is a cosmetic store. Zut has disappeared. Most of the ground floor of the site of the Cirque Medrano is a Carrefour supermarket. Where the Rat Mort stood is now a building housing a branch of the LCL bank. It's been through many changes but the basic shell of the Café de la Place Blanche is intact; it's now a Five Guys hamburger restaurant.

Strip clubs and prostitution still flourish in Montmartre and Pigalle, and criminality associated with the vice trade is rife. In addition, Pigalle has a modern way to monetise sexual desire involving plastic and batteries: shops like Sexodrome (which sounds like a David Lynch film, but is actually a huge sex toy superstore on three floors).

In 2019, I spent a month living above a sex club on the boulevard de Clichy. Directly opposite was a Monoprix supermarket in a building that now stands on the site of the demolished nightclub L'Enfer. I went shopping in there, once every few days, usually in the bland light of the morning. I like to hold on to the thought that all of Montmartre's past is contained somewhere in its present, that Fernande Olivier, Modigliani, Josephine Baker, Jacqueline Lamba, Apollinaire, Lee Miller, Frédé Gérard, and Johnny Thunders are partying in some dimly lit room up some steep stairs somewhere. But at the check-out queue in Monoprix, nothing of the excitement of those nights at L'Enfer lingered in the air.

On other occasions, though, especially at night, you can turn a corner in Pigalle or Montmartre and time twists, and rolls back. Visit Madame Arthur on the right night, and you might find yourself in a riotous gin-fuelled event hosted by Sophie Morello, the queen of the lesbian DJs, described by one of her friends as having 'un cœur aussi large qu'un cortège de révolutionnaires' ('a heart as wide as a procession of revolutionaries').

Sophie Morello's regulars throw themselves on top of each other, creating a Sapphic pyramid that doesn't quite reach the ceiling, then, onstage, a lesbian

in a gorilla costume reads 19th-century French love poetry. Just down the hill from the site of the Bateau-Lavoir, cigarette smokers and whisky drinkers crowd outside a bar booming out John Lee Hooker. Other music
is coming from under an unremarkable door opposite
where Van Gogh lived on rue Lepic; the signs of another late-night party in the hidden workshops behind
the estate agency. Lock eyes with the greatest dancer, a
bottle of something special comes out, the extravagant
dresser turns heads, an anarchist picks up a guitar. The
rhythm of the night takes hold, a rhythm centuries old;
the noise, the bodies of strangers close, the dance, the
party, the potential. You meet a poet on the walk home
as dawn breaks. A new day. Apollinaire is waiting. He's
talking Italian. You're in the zone. You'll wake up, eyes
and mind blurry, but with a determination to never let
the adventure end.

ORIGINAL ILLUSTRATION & COVER DESIGN
Zoë McLean, Manchester
zoe@confingopublishing.uk

TYPESETTING
John Oakey, Penrith
johnoakey1@gmail.com

BODY TYPE
*Minion 3, an updated and expanded version of
Robert Slimbach's early 90s design for Adobe.*

COVER TYPE
*Futura PT, developed at ParaType in 1995 by Vladimir
Yefimov, expands on the classic geometric sans-serif
typeface Futura designed by Paul Renner in 1927.*

'I loved every second of this read! A book littered with truth and adventure at every turn'
Emma Aylett

My Second Home: Sylvia Plath in Paris, 1956

'Delicately balanced between light and dark and inspiringly researched'
Shaun Tomkiss

'It is absolutely beautiful, the last few pages nearly brought me to tears. It is such a moving and unique account'
Rosie Day

All You Need is Dynamite: Acid, the Angry Brigade, and the End of the Sixties

'A highly enthralling, enchanting story... it's dynamite'
Ryan Walker

'An important piece of work - it was a pleasure to spend time with it'
John McCready

Not All Roses: The Life & Times of Stephen Cresser

'A brilliant short read and a moving, and evocative, piece of writing'
John Harris

'Really beautiful. Honest brutal gentle and very moving but there's hope too'
Luke Unabomber

CŌNFINGŌ

confingopublishing.uk